Learn How to Play the Classical Way

ASAP

Classical

GUITAR DUETS

BY JAMES DOUGLAS ESMOND

ISBN 978-1-57424-284-3
SAN 683-8022

Cover by James Creative Group

Copyright © 2012 CENTERSTREAM Publishing, LLC
P.O. Box 17878 - Anaheim Hills, CA 92817

www.centerstream-usa.com

ASAP Classical Guitar Duets
Table of contents and CD track list

Biography
James Douglas Esmond

James Douglas Esmond started playing the guitar in his teens. He received his Bachelor's of Music Theory and Classical Guitar performance from Ithaca College, Ithaca, N.Y. Upon graduating he became involved in church music. He has held positions in various churches, as a guitarist, organist, singer and conductor. In addition to his church work, he also teaches Guitar and Piano at Blue Sky Studios in Delmar, N.Y., and writes and arranges compositions in various genres and styles. He currently serves as the Organist/Music Director at Newtonville Methodist Church in Loudonville, N.Y. He resides in Albany N.Y. with his wife Meighan and daughter Evelyn. You can visit him on the web at: www.jdesmondmusic.com.

Foreword

I certainly believe this to be true and also believe that so much more can be done with the addition of a second guitar - both in terms of the range of the music possible and the flexibility for the musical texture, that it is too wonderful a genre to pass up. I have chosen to arrange a variety of Baroque, Classical and Romantic period pieces which all benefit from having this instrumentation. In these arrangements, I think players will also find that the reading level will be easier and that will be a benefit as well. These could be great pieces for the instructor looking to pair up students to work on many issues such as tone, dynamics and flexibility of tempo, in addition to refining their reading and technique. Whatever the use, I hope all will enjoy!

About the CD

All the pieces in this book have been recorded by myself, recording one part and then the other on top. I have, for the latter 6 pieces, included these in separate parts along with the full recording to better help the guitarist hear what they have to do. For these more challenging pieces it would be possible to use the CD as sort of a "rehearsal partner" when another guitarist is not present. If playing the Guitar 1 part listen to part 2, in addition to the full recording, to get familiar with it and then try to play to the CD. Also, it can be good just to listen to your part separately a lot for these later pieces.

Gymnopedie No.3

Eric Satie
arr. by J.Douglas Esmond

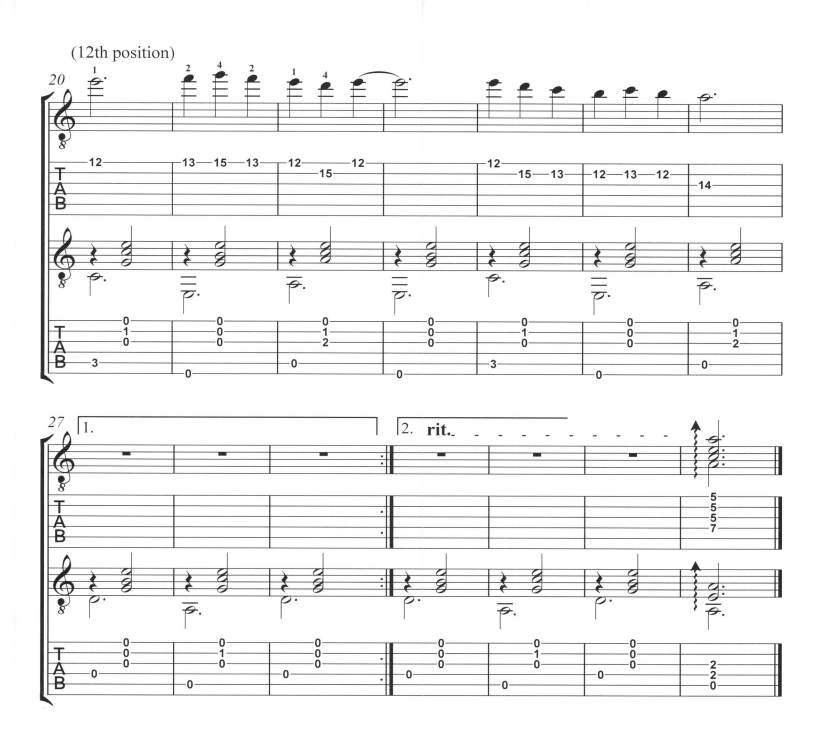

Italian Song

Pyotr Ilich Tchaikovsky
arr. by J.Douglas Esmond

10

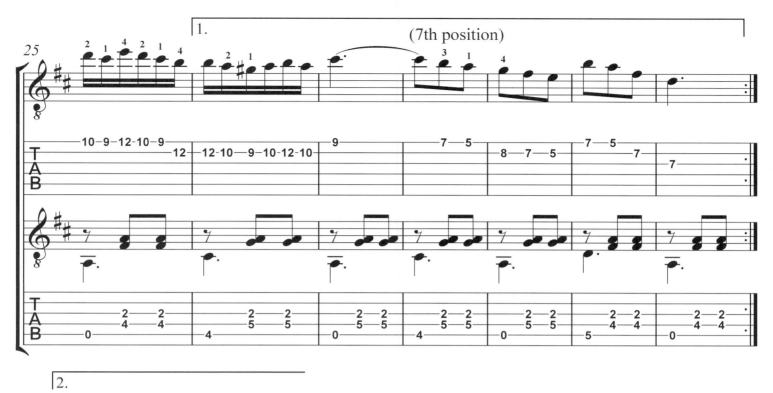

(7th position)

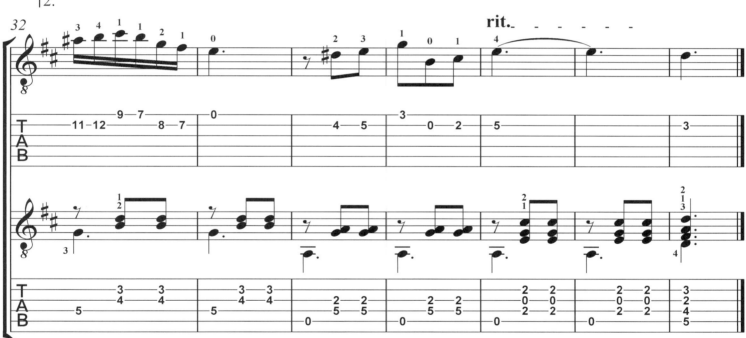

Sonatina
(Movt.1 - Moderato)

L.V.Beethoven
arr. by J.Douglas Esmond

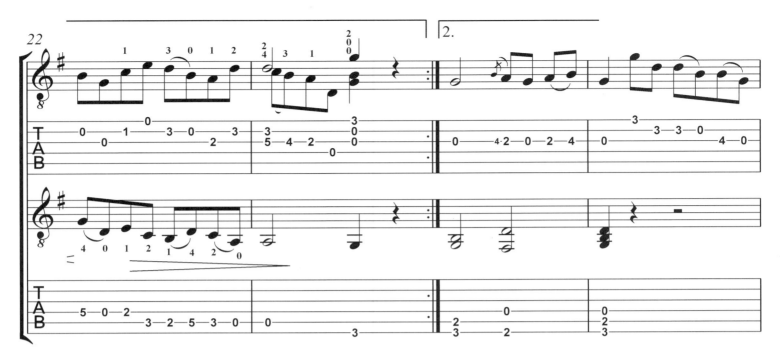

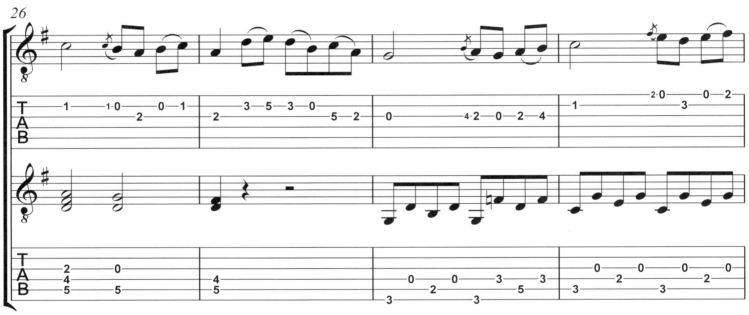

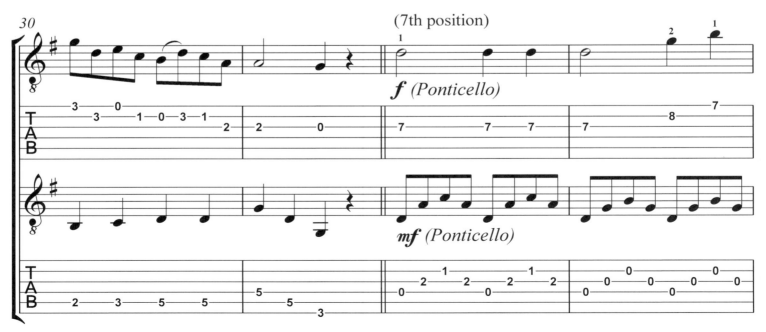

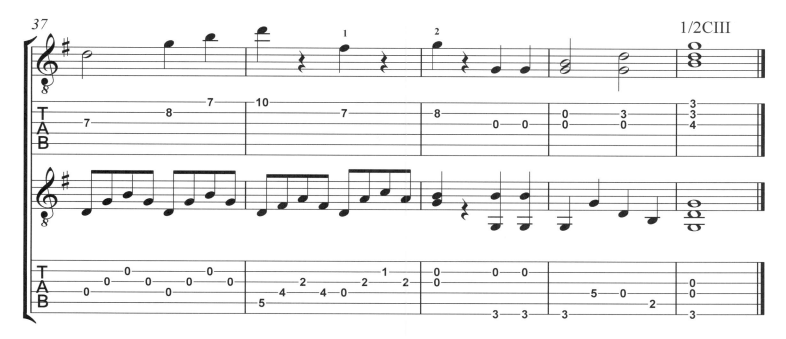

Ave Verum

Tarantella

Ballade

Friedrich Burgmuller
arr. by J.Douglas Esmond

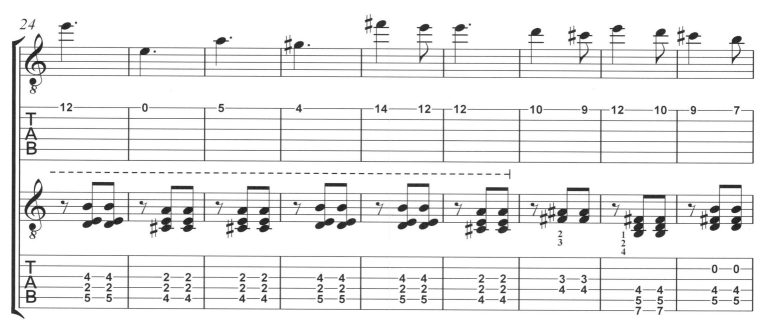

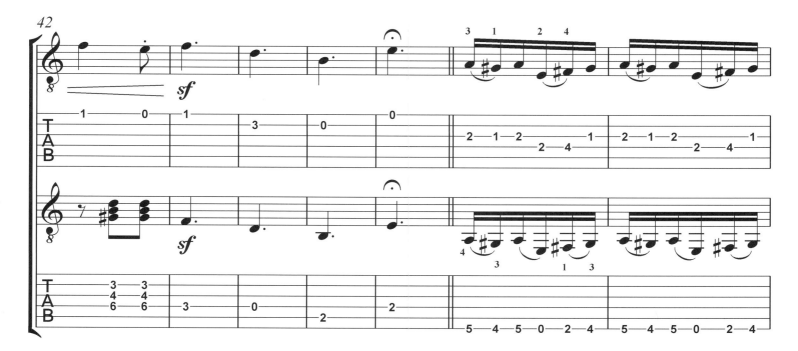

Friedrich Burgmueller

December 4, 1806 - February 13, 1874

He was born in Regensburg, Germany. Both his father, August, and his brother, Norbert, were musicians. His father was a musical theatre director in Weimar and other Southern German centers. After years of studies with Ludwig Spohr and Moritz Hauptmann, Friedrich moved to Paris in 1832, where he stayed until his death. There, he adopted Parisian music and developed his trademark, light style of playing. He wrote many pieces of salon music for the piano and published several albums. Burgmüller also went on to compose piano études intended for children. They are popular to this day.

Selections from his Opp. 68, 76, 100, 105 and 109 etudes and his Ballade appear in a wide variety of educational collections. In addition to these piano pieces, he composed works without opus numbers including variations, waltzes, nocturnes and polonaises. He composed stage works and two ballets, La Péri and Lady Harriet.

His most performed piece is the so-called Peasant Pas de Deux added to Adolphe Adam's ballet Giselle for its 1841 premiere. This music was originally titled Souvenirs de Ratisbonne, and is still performed today in every production of Giselle.

Prelude in E minor
(Op.28, no.4)

arr. by J.Douglas Esmond

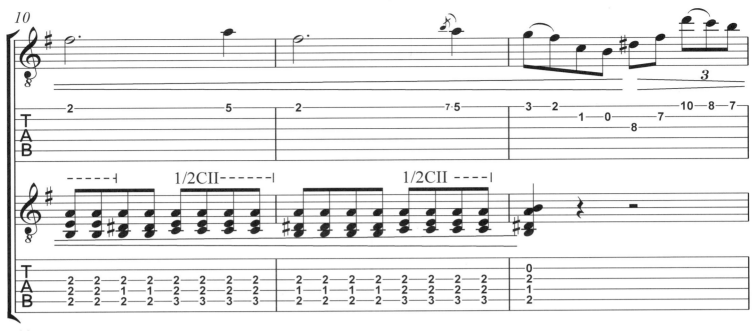

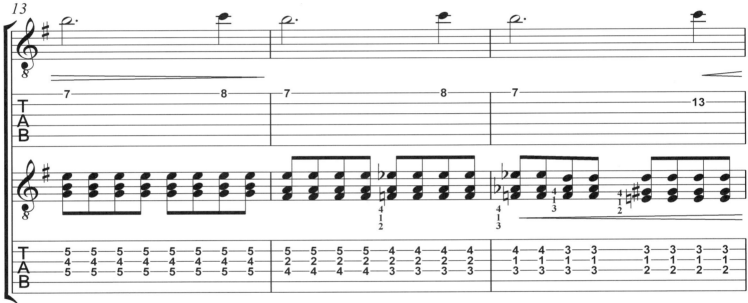

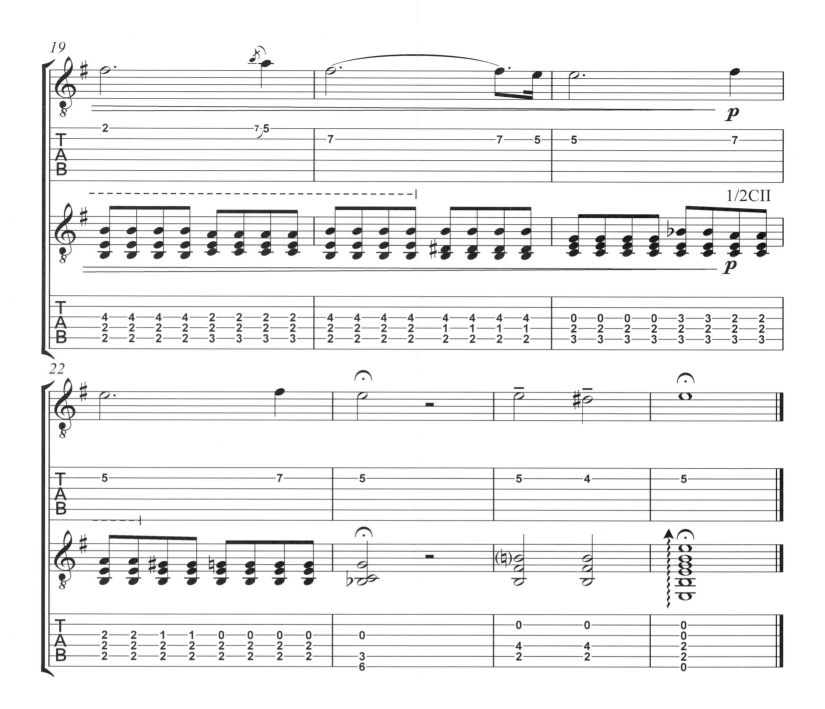

Traumerie

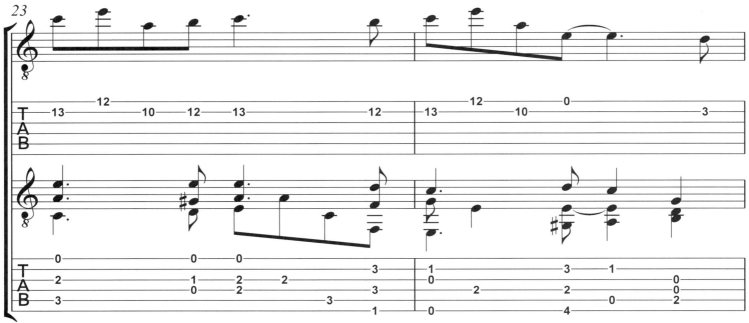

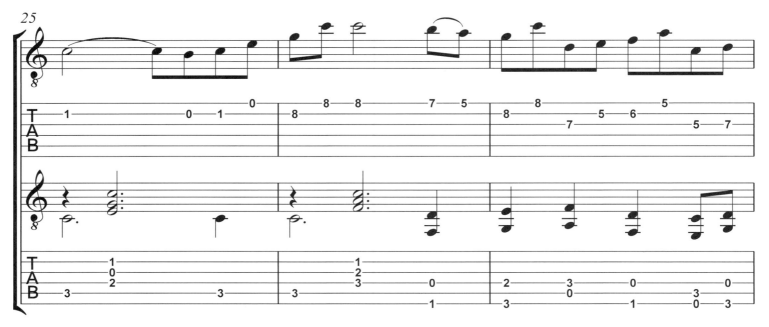

The Blue Danube

Johann Strauss
arr. by J.Douglas Esmond

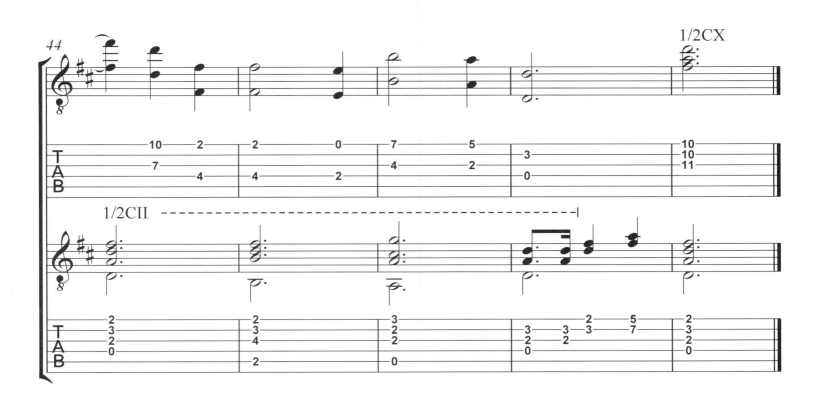

Johann Strauss II

October 25, 1825 – June 3, 1899

Johann Strauss II, also known as Johann Baptist Strauss or Johann Strauss, Jr., the Younger, or the Son (German: Sohn), was an Austrian composer of light music, particularly dance music and operettas. He composed over 500 waltzes, polkas, quadrilles, and other types of dance music, as well as several operettas and a ballet. In his lifetime, he was known as "The Waltz King", and was largely then responsible for the popularity of the waltz in Vienna during the 19th century.

Strauss was born in St. Ulrich (now a part of Neubau), the son of Johann Strauss I, another composer of dance music. His father did not wish him to become a composer, but rather a banker; however, the son defied his father's wishes, and went on to study music with the composer Joseph Drechsler and the violin with Anton Kollmann, the ballet répétiteur of the Vienna Court Opera. Strauss had two younger brothers, Josef and Eduard Strauss, who became composers of light music as well, although they were never as well known as their elder brother.

Some of Johann Strauss's most famous works include The Blue Danube, Kaiser-Walzer, Tales from the Vienna Woods, the Tritsch-Tratsch-Polka, and the Pizzicato Polka. Among his operettas, Die Fledermaus and Der Zigeunerbaron are the most well-known.

Sheep may safely graze
(from Cantata no.208)

J.S.Bach
arr. by J.Douglas Esmond

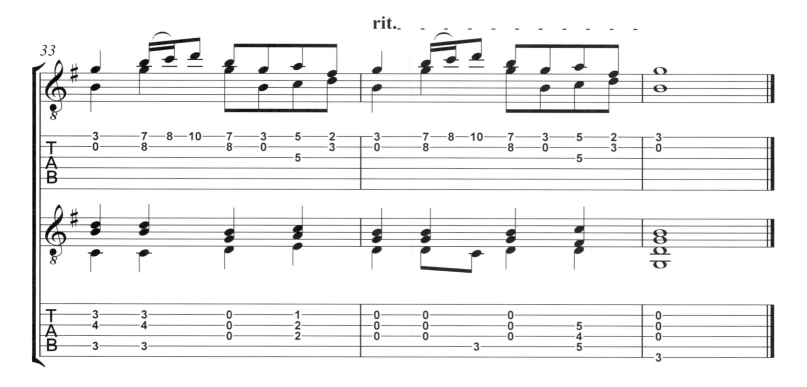

Johann Sebastian Bach

March 31,1685 – July 28, 1750

German composer, organist, harpsichordist, violist, and violinist of the
Baroque Period. He enriched many established German styles through his skill
in counterpoint, harmonic and motivic organisation, and the adaptation of
rhythms, forms, and textures from abroad, particularly from Italy and France.
Bach wrote much music, which was revered for its intellectual depth, technical
command, and artistic beauty. Many of his works are still known today, such as
the Brandenburg Concertos, the Mass in B minor, the Well-Tempered Clavier,
and his cantatas, chorales, partitas, passions, and organ works.

Bach was born in Eisenach, Saxe-Eisenach into a very musical family; his father, Johann Ambrosius
Bach was the director of the town's musicians, and all of his uncles were professional musicians. His
father taught him to play violin and harpsichord, and his brother, Johann Christoph Bach taught him
the clavichord, and exposed him to much contemporary music. Bach also sang, and he went to the St
Michael's School in Lüneburg, because of his skill in voice. After graduating, he held several musical
posts across Germany; he served as Kapellmeister (director of music) to Leopold, Prince of Anhalt-
Köthen, Cantor of Thomasschule in Leipzig, and Royal Court Composer to August III.   Bach's health
and vision declined in 1749, and he died on 28 July 1750. Modern historians believe that his death was
caused by a combination of stroke and pneumonia.

Bach's abilities as an organist were highly respected throughout Europe during his lifetime, although
he was not widely recognised as a great composer until a revival of interest and performances of his
music in the first half of the 19th century. He is now generally regarded as one of the main composers of
the Baroque period, and as one of the greatest composers of all time.

More Great Guitar Books from Centerstream...